THE
FOLK
STENCIL BOOK

A UNIQUE COLLECTION OF READY-TO-USE STENCILS
IN CLASSIC DESIGNS BY

LOUISE DRAYTON
JANE THOMSON

HOW TO BEGIN PP. 2–7

TROPICAL AFRICAN PP. 8–11

DESERT AFRICAN PP. 12–15

MOORISH PP. 16-19

NATIVE AMERICAN PP. 20–23

MAYAN & AZTEC PP. 24-27

MIX & MATCH PP. 28–31

DORLING KINDERSLEY
London • New York • Sydney • Moscow

How to Begin

STENCILLING IS AN ANCIENT DECORATIVE technique and is easy to master. Once you understand how to do it, you will find that stencilling a pattern takes very little time. First, choose your design. Then measure the surface you want to stencil and decide how and where to use the pattern. Experiment with different colours and backgrounds to give your design another look, and try masking and combining other motifs with your stencil to build a unique design. You can use your stencils just about anywhere, and – with a little imagination – create hundreds of designs.

STARTING TO STENCIL

BEFORE YOU BEGIN any project, start with a simple design and practise on lining paper. Begin with the dry stages: gather the equipment you will need, and then cut your sponges and stencils. Mask the edges of the stencil. Next, the wet stages: experiment with paint consistency and sponging, then practise dabbing on scrap paper.

LINING PAPER

LARGE RULER

PLUMB LINE

HOME-MADE PLUMB LINE

Make your own plumb line with a small weight and string

SET SQUARE

EMULSION

METALLIC PAINT

SOLVENT

TUBE ACRYLIC

FABRIC MEDIUM

SCISSORS

TRACING PAPER

SCRAP PAPER

MASKING TAPE

SCALPEL

SPIRIT LEVELS

DENSE FOAM SPONGES

STUCCO PAINT AND SPATULA

ACRYLICS

CERAMIC PAINTS

ERASER

SOFT PENCILS

PAINT BRUSHES

TAPE MEASURE

PERMANENT PENS

PAINT DISHES

STENCILLING EQUIPMENT

Stencilling tools include a pair of scissors, sponge, tape, ruler, pen, soft pencils, paper, paint and dish, and paint brush. More complex projects need additional materials.

Make sure the dome is smooth and even

1 Cut the sponge into 35-mm and 65-mm (1½-in and 2½-in) squares; trim off the tops to create a smooth dome shape. Make a few smaller domes for fine detail.

2 Working on a flat surface, trace the guidelines from the page behind each plastic stencil sheet with a permanent-ink pen; cut out and number each stencil.

3 Tape strips of tracing paper 5 cm (2 in) wide to each side to prevent paint from smudging over your surface. Cover parts of the stencil you will not need (see p.6).

Watery paint will drip off your sponge and can ruin your stencil design

The paint should be the consistency of cream

Too much thick paint makes a dense, heavy colour with no pattern marks from the sponge

Watery paint creates a washed-out colour with small bubbles

This paint is at the right consistency to produce a textured pattern

4 *It is very important that your paint is mixed to a creamy consistency. Bottled acrylics should be about right, but you may have to thin other types of paint.*

5 *Test the consistency of your paints by dabbing the sponge lightly onto scrap paper. Paint of the right consistency will produce an evenly stippled texture.*

WATERY PAINT

The paint shown here is too watery and, because it has seeped under the stencil, all the details are lost – a disastrous result.

The easiest way to apply paint is to dip the sponge into the dish

This paint has not been worked evenly into the sponge, producing a blotchy texture

Coverage is better, but dabbing on the same spot would work the paint in

This paint has been applied well and the texture is uniform

6 *Apply a little paint to the rounded dome of a dry sponge. There are two ways to do this. You can dab the sponge lightly into a dish of paint, or use a brush to coat the sponge.*

7 *Before doing your stencil, dab the sponge onto scrap paper to work in all the excess paint. Dab gently in one area, and then below to test.*

8 *The sponge dome must be smooth and evenly coated with paint to produce an even texture with no blotches.*

Each time you add more paint to the sponge, re-test the distribution of paint

Make sure the paint is dry before repositioning the stencil

9 *Tape down the stencil on lining or scrap paper to practise. Dab a sponge over the whole pattern with the first colour; use a clean, dry sponge for the second colour to add depth or to pick out areas of detail.*

10 *When you have applied all your chosen colours, slowly peel back the stencil to check paint texture and distribution.*

USING YOUR STENCILS

Choosing a pattern is the first step in using your stencils. Decide where you want to use your design, and select your colour scheme. Do you want a bold all-over pattern, a bright picture rail, or a striking motif to act as a focal point in a room? Depending on your choices, you may need to master a variety of techniques, such as measuring, repeating, and mitring. After you have completed a project, clean your stencils, repair any damage, and store the stencils flat for the next use. With care, your stencils will last for a long time, and can be used again and again.

MEASURING THE PATTERN

Before you apply a pattern to any surface, stencil a sample on lining paper as a guide. Mark the centre line and the base-line of the main part of the design on the lining paper, then mark and measure the distance to the pattern's repeat.

Mark the horizontal base-line of the main part of the design — use a spirit level to help you keep the pattern even

This distance is the pattern repeat length

Use a plumb line to keep the stencil true

The gap here is narrower than usual

Stretch the pattern from the repeat line

SPACING THE PATTERN

Measure your surface and work out the number of repeats. Avoid stencilling on a corner by adding space between the repeats.

CLOSING UP THE PATTERN

You may need to alter the pattern to make it fit your surface; to include more repeats, close up the space between them.

STRETCHING THE PATTERN

Leave wider gaps between parts of the stencil or between repeats to stretch it; these gaps should be the same throughout the design.

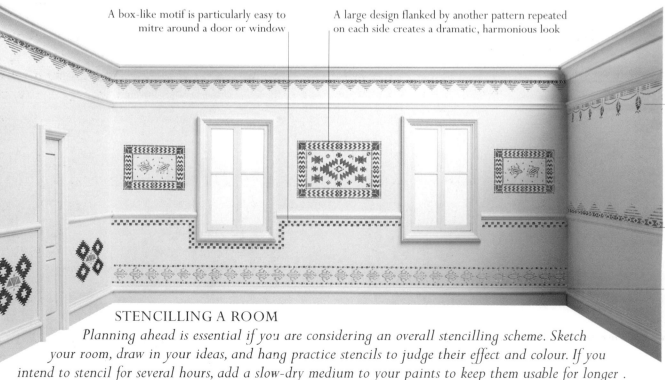

A box-like motif is particularly easy to mitre around a door or window

A large design flanked by another pattern repeated on each side creates a dramatic, harmonious look

Stencil a continuous border just below the ceiling if you want to make it seem lower

Use an existing picture rail as a guide for positioning your design — or stencil a picture rail

Repeat a bold design around a door or in a hallway; vary the height to suit the space

Create a dado and enliven a room with a stencil placed about 90 cm (3 ft) above the floorboards

Make the most of skirting-boards by stencilling a bright pattern just above them

STENCILLING A ROOM

Planning ahead is essential if you are considering an overall stencilling scheme. Sketch your room, draw in your ideas, and hang practice stencils to judge their effect and colour. If you intend to stencil for several hours, add a slow-dry medium to your paints to keep them usable for longer .

ALIGNING PATTERNS

If you need a vertical rule to align a stencil, hang a plumb line above the stencil area, place a ruler against the string, and draw a line with pencil or chalk; erase the line later.

TESTING COLOURWAYS

Check that you like the colours for your design by stencilling onto a sample of your wall colour or wallpaper. Depending on the background, colours can appear different.

EQUAL SPACING

Position a second stencil so that the tracing-paper mask around the stencil overlaps the first. Trace a few lines. Stencil, place the third stencil, and match tracings with the second.

MITRING

Place the set square at the point where horizontal and vertical base-lines intersect

Slightly overlap the previous stencil to ensure there is no gap between the mitred elements of the design

Successful mitring depends on the two base-lines being accurately drawn at a 90° angle

1 Working from pencilled base-lines, use a set square to position a tracing-paper mask at 45° across the end of the stencil. Tape it to the stencil, and dab in paint.

2 Finish the horizontal pattern, then blot the stencil, keeping the mask in place. Flip the stencil, position it on the vertical base-line, and dab in paint.

3 Carefully peel back the stencil when the paint is dry. After you remove the stencil, rub out the horizontal and vertical base-lines with a very soft eraser.

CARING FOR YOUR STENCILS

Stencils are delicate and need to be handled with care. Remove tape and masks gently, and clean the stencils after each use. The inked numbers may rub off, so renew them as needed. Store each stencil flat between sheets of paper.

1 Clean off dried acrylic paints with methylated spirits. Use a paint brush to ease off the paint.

2 Soak the stencils in warm soapy water, and rinse in clean water. Dry them flat between light cotton towels.

REPAIRING DAMAGED STENCILS

Some of the stencil designs are very intricate, and they may develop small rips or tears if the stencils are not handled properly. This type of damage is easy to repair.

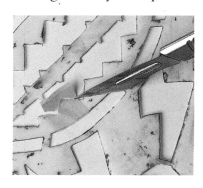

1 Start by covering the tear on both sides of the stencil with masking tape. Be sure the stencil is perfectly flat.

2 Using a scalpel or craft knife, carefully cut along the edge of the design. Peel away any excess tape.

PAINT EFFECTS

How you use your paints will completely transform the look of your stencils. Mixing colours is fun and easy – use a brush to blend them, and keep a record of the quantities you use. Try blending, highlighting, and shading, and experiment to achieve the style that suits you best.

This design has been stencilled as though the light source is from underneath

BLENDING COLOURS

1 Start by sponging the base colour, which should be the lightest shade, over your first stencil. Apply the paint evenly, then add extra colour to areas of fine detail.

2 Use a clean, dry sponge for your next colour to avoid muddying the paints. Stipple the second deeper colour lightly over the first coat; blend towards the edges.

3 When the paint is dry, remove the first stencil. If you use additional stencils, repeat Steps 1 and 2; try to match the colour density and tone of the first stencil.

MASKING A STENCIL

The simplest way to create a mask is to tape a piece of tracing paper over the part of the design you will not be using. Masking allows you to isolate part of a design or colour areas that need to be distinct, to simplify a complicated pattern, or to substitute one part of a stencil for another.

ADDING TEXTURE

Paint mixed with a texture medium

A special medium, usually available as a gel, can be mixed in with your paint to create textured effects. Because the paint is now thicker, it is easier to apply with a small spatula instead of a brush.

SIMPLE MASKING

A sheet of straight-edged paper makes an effective mask – here, a row of diamonds has been covered to create triangles

1 Start by covering the part of the design you want to mask with tracing paper. Secure the paper with tape.

2 Place the stencil in position and dab in paints. When the paint is dry, gently remove the stencil.

THREE-IN-ONE MASKING

1 Some stencils in this book have three parts – two inner elements and an outer frame. Label the inner parts; use a scalpel to cut the bridges away from the outer frame.

2 Remove one of the inner elements (here, part B) to expose the area that will be filled with colour. Secure part A to the outer stencil frame with tape, position, and stencil.

3 Peel back the stencil. There will now be an empty space where part A was. To fill it with colour, remove A from the outer frame, attach B, reposition the frame, and stencil.

STENCILLING ON OTHER MATERIALS

Almost any surface can be stencilled – from bare plaster walls to fabric, wood, ceramics, and glass. All of these can be sponged with acrylic or specialist paints (follow the manufacturer's instructions carefully; some ceramic paints may need to be baked). Areas that need to be protected can be varnished.

FABRICS

Stencil onto fabrics such as silk, muslin, or cotton

PAINT CONSISTENCY
Do not thin the paint you use on fabrics, as it is easier to use when thick. To prevent bleeding, add a commercial fabric medium.

USING BLOTTERS
When stencilling lightweight or sheer fabrics, such as muslin or silk, use a blotter of absorbent paper or remnants beneath the fabric in case the paint soaks through.

WOODS

Bare wood   Primer and undercoat   Emulsion/acrylic base coat

Seal the stencil with clear varnish if extra protection is needed

Seal the board with wood primer and an undercoat, then stencil with acrylic or emulsion paints

BARE WOOD
Prepare the wood surface with sandpaper or wire wool, and wipe clean. Stencil the design. If you want a richly coloured, polished effect, treat the wood with beeswax after stencilling.

PAINTED WOOD
Sand the wood before you begin. Prime it, sand the surface, paint an undercoat, then sand again. Brush after each sanding. Paint the background colour; when dry, stencil your design.

CERAMICS, METAL, AND GLASS

GLASS
Stencil directly onto clean glass with ceramic paints. Fingerprints or any tape residues will prevent the paint from adhering properly.

UNGLAZED CERAMICS
Unglazed ceramics, such as terracotta pots or tiles, can be stencilled with acrylic paints.

GLAZED CERAMICS
Stencil directly onto glazed surfaces with ceramic paints (follow the manufacturer's instructions). Ceramic tiles can be stencilled either in place or when "loose" (before they have been fitted). If loose, line the tiles up, number them, and tape closely together; this will make positioning the painted tiles much easier.

METAL
Metallic surfaces – tin buckets, for example – can be painted with ceramic paints. With care, the design will last.

TROPICAL AFRICAN

SOME OF THE OLDEST DESIGNS of this region — highly stylized, geometrical shapes, and depictions of animal bodies, markings, or tracks — are found on rock paintings, and are still used. Grids and squares were common, and found on goatskin or leather cushions as well as other household items, such as brass dishes, gourds, and baskets. Sometimes even stones and large seeds were decorated. Certain designs had special meanings, and were painted on the body and on houses to signify a person's identity or status, or for protection. In this environment, the calabash tree played a singular role: its large fruit was hollowed out, decorated, and used to store liquids, while the wood was cut and carved into stamping blocks for decorating fabric.

Make sure that the first stencil of any pattern sits in position — use a spirit level to draw the horizontal line

1 Mask off the left end of Stencil 6 (see "Masking a Stencil", p.6). Use a pencil or soft chalk to mark a horizontal line and vertical line in the area to be painted, and begin to stencil at the top left-hand corner.

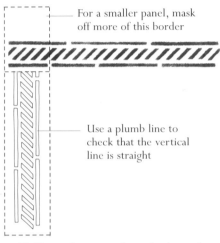

For a smaller panel, mask off more of this border

Use a plumb line to check that the vertical line is straight

2 Turn the stencil, and place the masked end at a right angle to the top stencil. Place a set square over the stencil to check the angle, and reposition if necessary.

Any gaps between different motifs should be uniform throughout the entire design

3 Position the zebra stripes (Stencil 4) in the left-hand corner. You can enlarge the design by widening the gap between the stripes and the border.

4 After completing the stripes, stencil the border pattern to the right. Mask each end of the border pattern, place to fit between the two vertical borders, and stencil.

The chequered square should be placed to the right and then below the leopard spots

5 Dab in the leopard spots (Stencil 3) to the right of the border. Let the stencil dry, then dab more spots below the stripes. Stencil another vertical border.

You can combine stencils, and use them on odd shapes, such as a lampbase. The stencils are flexible and can bend around curves.

Finish the panel with Stencil 6 along the base-line

1

2

Trace the guidelines from this page onto the plastic stencil sheet with a permanent pen. Cut along the vertical line of perforations that attaches the sheet to the book. Cut out and number each stencil. Place each one on card before removing any remaining infills with a scalpel.

3

4

5

6

TROPICAL AFRICAN VARIATIONS

BORDER (YORUBA TRIBE): STENCILS 4, 5

Begin with Stencil 5, then cut a mask to cover part of Stencil 4 and dab in paint

LEAF FRIEZE (KUBA TRIBE): STENCILS 2, 4

Cut an oval mask to cover the turtle's body (Stencil 2), place on stripes (Stencil 4), and stencil; mask off turtle legs and head, and stencil in empty oval

BEADED BORDER: STENCILS 1, 3

TURTLE TRACKS: STENCIL 6

MOTIF BORDER: STENCILS 3, 5

CHEQUERED BORDER: STENCIL 1

SQUARE PANEL: STENCILS 1, 3, 4, 6

Stencil this panel on a cushion cover, or enlarge it for a bedspread

TURTLE FRIEZE: STENCILS 1, 2, 5

Pencil a horizontal line, and place the stripe of the turtle's back on this line

MIXED MOTIF BORDER (YORUBA TRIBE): STENCILS 5, 31

Mask off the upper half of Stencil 31

Try using this stencil above Stencil 5 as well as below

DIAMOND TURTLE FRIEZE (MOMTOR TRIBE): STENCILS 2, 3, 30

Use the same colour as the spots, but dab in less paint for a faded look

TRIANGLE BORDER (ASHANTI TRIBE): STENCIL 4, 31

Mask off a triangular area of Stencil 4

DESERT AFRICAN

THE HARSH CONDITIONS OF THE DESERT have made life difficult for people living there, and many have been nomads for centuries. Traders from the Arabian peninsula established caravan routes across the Sahara through an area that now covers Algeria, Tunisia, and Morocco, bringing artifacts and design motifs with them. Outside a few larger settlements, people lived in tents, which protected them from the sun, the wind, and the cold nights. Textiles woven on hand-looms were made into woollen tent cloths, rugs, wall hangings, and blankets; these were often decorated with diamond shapes, triangles, and chevrons in broad horizontal bands. Some textiles incorporated gold and silver threads, and such valuable cloths would often form part of a bride's dowry.

Run the length of your border space with this stencil first

1 Mark a horizontal line (if working on a wall, use a spirit level). Mask off half the diamonds on Stencil 10. Place the stencil on the line, and dab with paint.

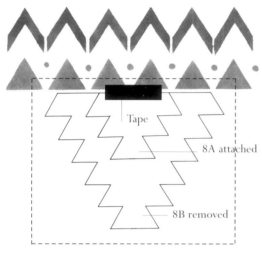

Tape
8A attached
8B removed

2 Remove 8B (the large stepped chevron) from Stencil 8; retain 8A with tape. Place under the border.

The finished motif

3 Stencil the large stepped chevron below the entire length of the border. When paint is dry, remove 8A from the stencil.

8B attached
Dab paint in this space

4 Reattach 8B with tape, and turn the entire stencil upside down. Stencil the small stepped chevron inside the larger one.

5 Finish off by turning Stencil 10 upside down, with the mask still in place, and stencil along the length of the border.

The dots in Stencil 10 look strong when highlighted in a colour that contrasts with the border

You can create translucent colours, such as those on the back wall, by adding an extender medium to the paint; this makes it thinner and clearer without becoming watery.

7

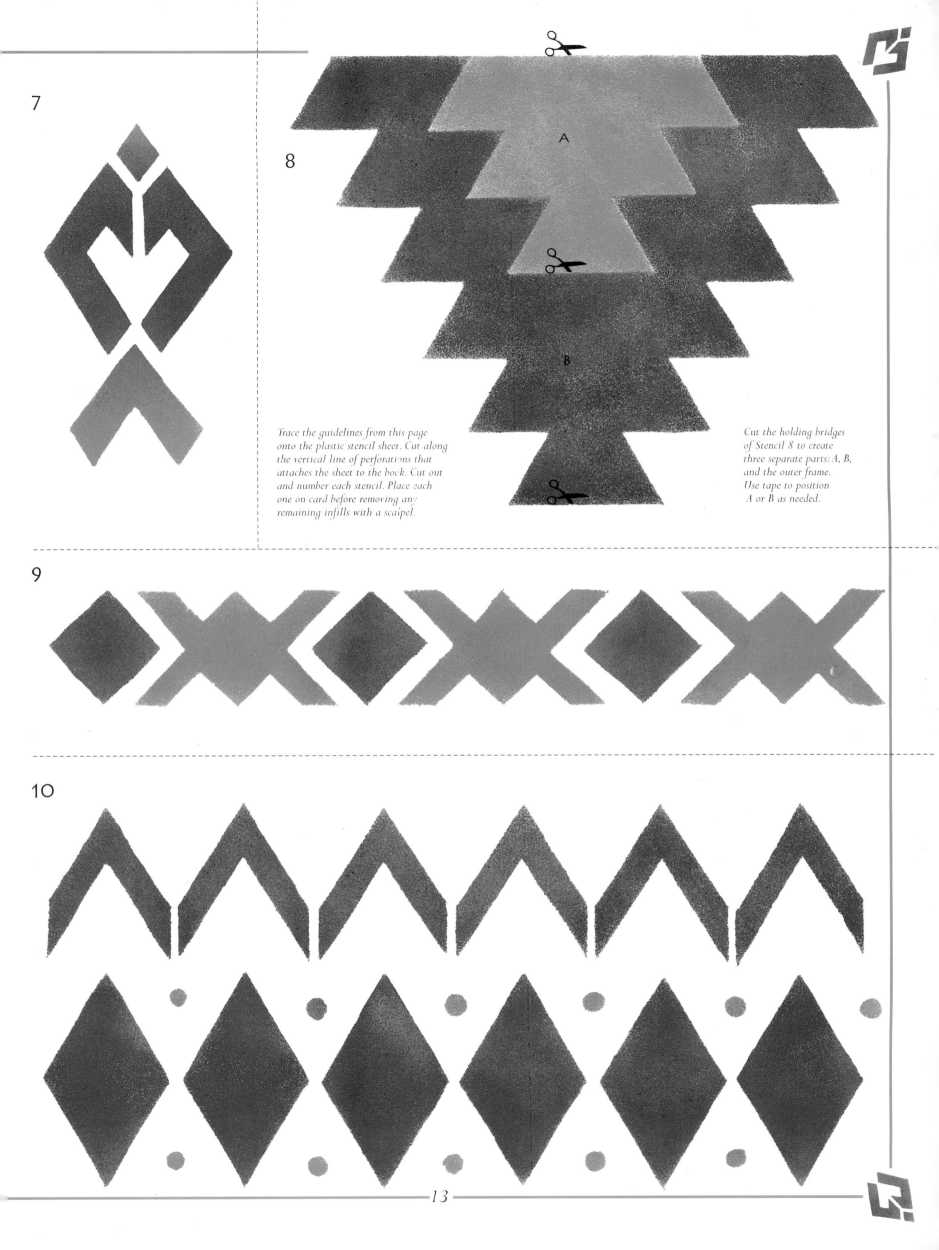

8

A

B

Trace the guidelines from this page onto the plastic stencil sheet. Cut along the vertical line of perforations that attaches the sheet to the book. Cut out and number each stencil. Place each one on card before removing any remaining infills with a scalpel.

Cut the holding bridges of Stencil 8 to create three separate parts: A, B, and the outer frame. Use tape to position A or B as needed.

9

10

DESERT AFRICAN VARIATIONS

FISHES: STENCIL 7

CHEVRON FRIEZE: STENCILS 8, 10

Position the outer frame of Stencil 8, then place 8B a few centimetres away; dab in paint to create the outline shape, then stencil in the mirror image

STEPPED CHEVRONS & TRIANGLES: STENCILS 8, 10

Choose a strong colour for the dots

DIAMOND ZIGZAGS: STENCIL 10

This design would create a striking border for a floor rug

Four-Fishes Square: Stencils 7, 10

Dots & Diamonds: Stencil 10

Braided Band: Stencil 9

Double Zigzags: Stencil 10

Mask off all but the points of the diamonds on Stencil 10 to create the frame

Dots & Triangles: Stencil 10

Diamonds & Crosses: Stencil 9

Linked Fishes: Stencil 7

Diamonds & Fishes: Stencils 7, 10

Crosses & Chevrons: Stencils 7, 8, 9

This frieze can be used upside down or right side up, or doubled for a very wide design

MOORISH

IN THE SEVENTH CENTURY, nomadic northern African tribes were conquered by an Islamic army from the Arab world. Their descendants, the Moors, invaded Spain in 711 and created a distinctive, sophisticated culture. Moorish art, governed by Islamic principles, generally prohibited the representation of divine or saintly personages, and focused instead on highly stylized and decorative elements. Intricate designs, many derived from Arabic calligraphy, were adapted for tiles, jewellery, and clothing. Architecture was and is a vital part of Islamic culture, and Moorish arches – a key structural feature – were often decorated with embroidered textiles. Tassels, a popular decorative element, were made from the loose ends of a woven cloth tied into a knot. They were often embellished with beads, and are found everywhere: on hangings, cushions, bags, clothing – even on the reins of horses and camels.

This design is extremely versatile and looks especially striking in rich colours. Try a gold or metallic paint to enrich the base colour.

Be sure to align the bases of the stencil on an even horizontal line

Make sure the repeat gaps are always the same; do not stretch too far, or the support will look weak

1 Using a spirit level, mark out a horizontal line on the wall with either pencil or chalk. Place both bases of Stencil 11 on this line, and dab in paint.

2 Continue to stencil the arches along the horizontal line, leaving a small gap between them. This gap can be increased if you want to stretch the design slightly.

3 Once you have completely finished all the arches, carefully position the support (Stencil 12) centrally just underneath the point where the arches join.

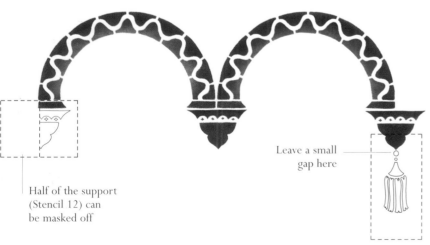

Half of the support (Stencil 12) can be masked off

Leave a small gap here

Shade the tassel on one side for a three-dimensional effect

4 If you want to finish the line of arches neatly – for example, in a corner – mask off one half of the support stencil.

5 Finish off the arches with the tassel motif. Place Stencil 15 just below the support and lightly dab in colour.

6 Use a plumb line if you want the tassels to hang straight, or position them at a slight angle to create a "windblown" effect.

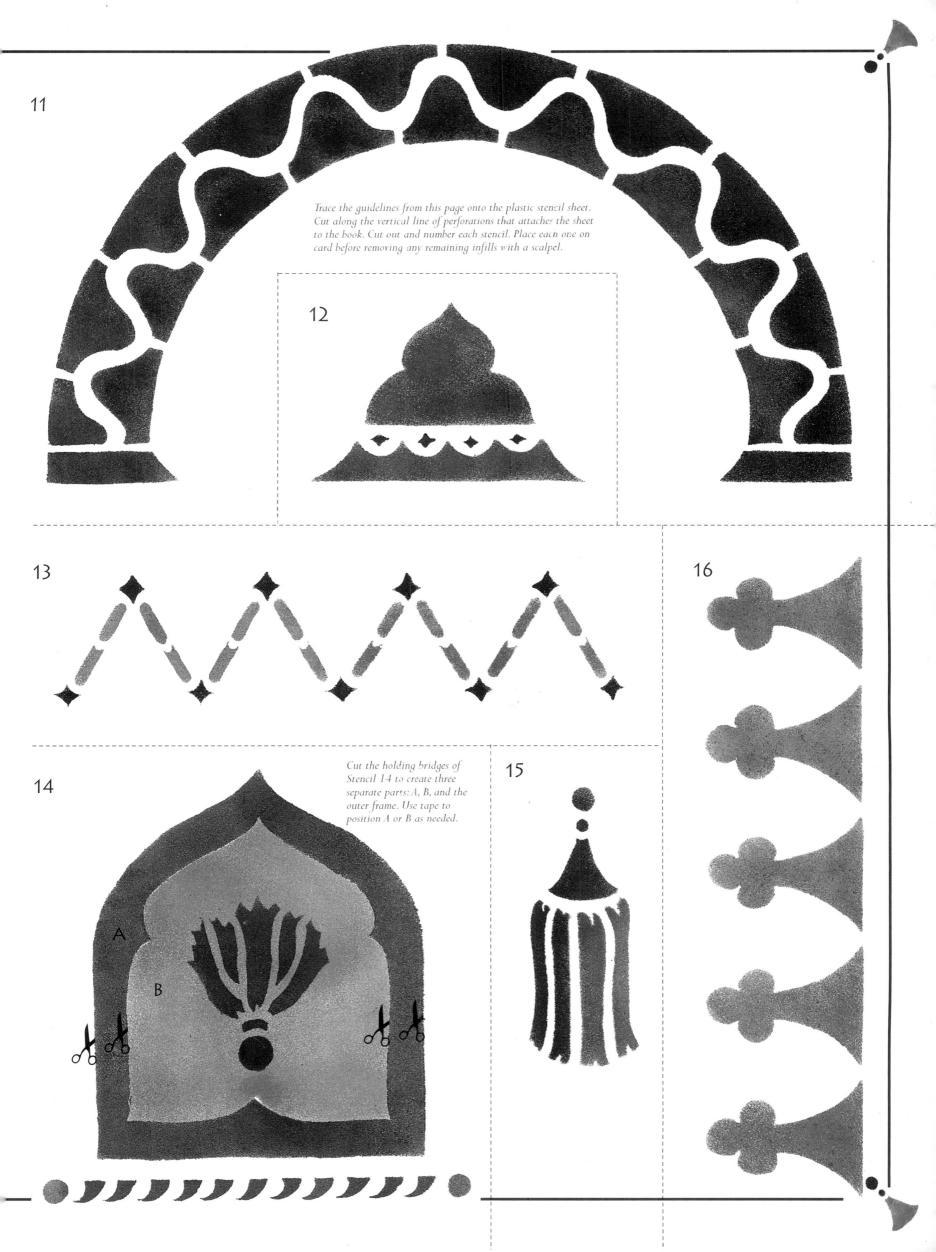

11

Trace the guidelines from this page onto the plastic stencil sheet. Cut along the vertical line of perforations that attaches the sheet to the book. Cut out and number each stencil. Place each one on card before removing any remaining infills with a scalpel.

12

13

16

Cut the holding bridges of Stencil 14 to create three separate parts: A, B, and the outer frame. Use tape to position A or B as needed.

14

A

B

15

Moorish Variations

Single-Pawn Border: Stencil 16

Try using this design above a skirting-board or mitre it around a picture frame

Double-Pawn Border: Stencil 16

This mirrored design, with its interesting negative (interior) shape, creates the illusion of window tracery

Bells & Tassels: Stencils 12, 15

Braided Shields & Tassels: Stencils 14, 14a, 14b, 15

This is an excellent design for a pelmet above a window

Triangles & Beaded Shields: Stencils 10, 13, 14, 14b

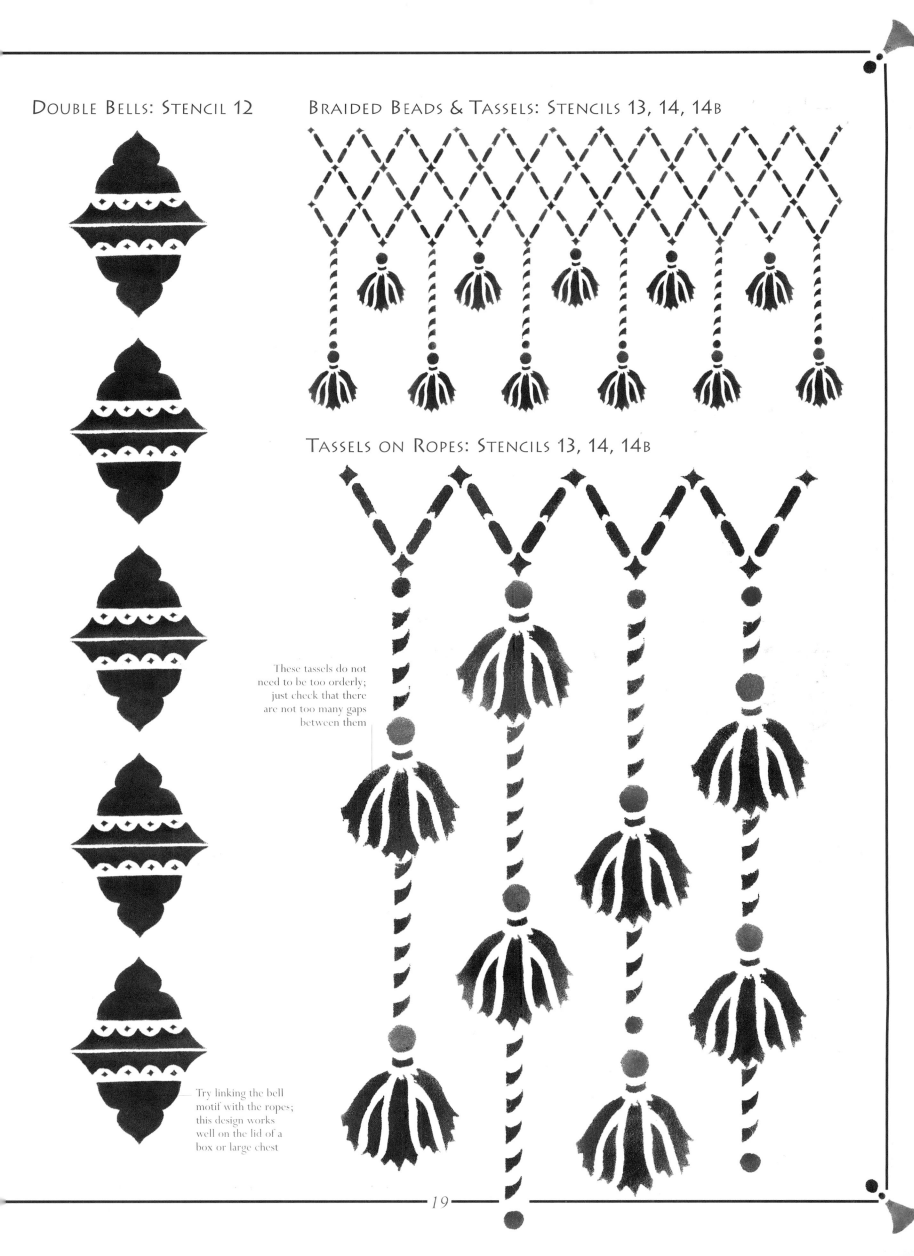

DOUBLE BELLS: STENCIL 12

BRAIDED BEADS & TASSELS: STENCILS 13, 14, 14B

TASSELS ON ROPES: STENCILS 13, 14, 14B

These tassels do not need to be too orderly; just check that there are not too many gaps between them

Try linking the bell motif with the ropes; this design works well on the lid of a box or large chest

NATIVE AMERICAN

About 20,000 years ago, during the last Ice Age, hunters from Siberia crossed a land bridge into Alaska and later dispersed to form more than 300 Native American tribes. Many, especially those of the western Great Basin and Great Plains, remained nomads, living in buffalo-hide tipis decorated with paints made from ground stones, vegetable dyes, and earth pigments. The porcupine quills used to sew tipis were also dyed and stitched onto saddlebags and clothing to create elaborate designs. Native American belief was based on a profound respect for nature, and one of the most revered animals was the eagle. Universally linked with solar deities and a symbol of authority, strength, and pride, the eagle was called Thunderbird; its feathers represented rays of the sun, and were attached to sacred ceremonial pipes, arrows, headdresses, and war shields.

When stencilling designs onto fabric, add a special medium to acrylic paints; quilt by hand or use a sewing machine to achieve a patchwork look.

Position carefully on the horizontal line marked out on the wall

1 Before painting the eagle frieze, practise on lining or scrap paper; check the size of the pattern and repeat to make sure it fits the wall. Place Stencil 17 on a pencilled horizontal line and create a border.

Position Stencil 19B in the centre of the outer frame of Stencil 19, and attach to the surface with double-sided tape | Remove 19A

2 Take Stencil 19 and place it just above the border. With double-sided tape, attach 19B in the centre. Stencil a row of diamonds along the border, making sure they are all the same distance apart.

3 Once you have completed one row of diamonds, make a second row just above the first, leaving the same gap between them as before. If you want a deeper frieze, stencil a third row of diamonds.

4 Mark a horizontal line above the diamonds, leaving the same space between the border and the diamonds as at the base of the frieze. Stencil the border.

Place the eagle motif between – but not touching – the diamonds

5 Now position the eagles (Stencil 21) in the spaces between the diamonds; pencil a horizontal line so that they line up evenly.

6 This is the completed eagle frieze, which would look striking on a wall or large chest. Experiment by combining the eagle and diamond with other stencils.

17

18

19

Cut the holding bridges of Stencil 19 to create three parts: A, B, and the outside frame. Use tape to reattach A or to fix B to your surface as needed.

20

21

Trace the guidelines from this page onto the plastic stencil sheet. Cut along the vertical line of perforations that attaches the sheet to the book. Cut out and number each stencil. Place each one on card before removing any remaining infills with a scalpel.

22

Native American Variations

Eagle Feather & Porcupine Quill Border: Stencils 18, 20

Keep the base-line level, but angle the feathers for a more natural look

Wide Tomahawk Border: Stencil 22

This is an effective design for a dado rail, or to create vertical wall panels

Eagle Feather Border: Stencil 20

Use this design as a vertical motif on curtains or walls

Tomahawk & Diamond Frieze: Stencils 17, 19, 19a, 19b, 22

Diamond Frieze: Stencils 9, 19

Position Stencil 19 on your surface, attach 19B (the small motif) in the centre, and dab in paint to create the large diamond

Boxed Diamond Frieze: Stencils 6, 19a, 30a

Attach Stencil 30A to the surface, place Stencil 19A in the centre with some double-sided tape or blue tack, then dab in a bright or contrasting colour in the centre

Tomahawk Border: Stencil 22

Mask Stencil 32 to create this design — change direction of the stripes at the midpoint of the border

Brow Band Border: Stencils 17, 32

Diamond & Porcupine Quill Border: Stencils 18, 19

Follow the instructions for the diamond frieze above, then remove 19B; reattach 19A inside the frame of Stencil 19 with tape, and dab in the small central motif

Mayan & Aztec

Until the sixteenth century, when they were overcome by the invading *conquistadores* from Spain, the Mayan and Aztec tribes dominated Central America. Their powerful, hierarchical culture derived from older Amerindian tribes who had been building stone and adobe stepped pyramids in the region from about 1800 BC; these buildings are the source of the recurring step motif. One tribe, the Toltecs, built stone temples at Tula that are remarkable for the way in which are they fitted together without cement. All these cultures held elaborate religious festivals for their hundreds of gods. Their ceremonial costumes incorporated gems, parrot feathers, and the long, streaming tailfeathers of the quetzal bird associated with a major deity, Quetzalcoatl, the plumed serpent god of wisdom. The torches that were used in these ceremonies are another popular motif.

These stencils have been used on natural woven baskets. Try using them on rush mats or cane blinds.

Position carefully on the horizontal line marked out on the wall

Shade around the edges of Stencil 25

The finished plume and dots

You could also use a vibrant, contrasting colour for this motif

1 *Using a spirit level, mark out a horizontal line on the wall. Mask off the central plume motif on Stencil 25, place the stencil on the line, and dab in colour.*

2 *Continue to stencil the step motif along the horizontal line, leaving a small gap between the two. This gap can be increased if you want to stretch the design.*

3 *Once you have completed the border, mask off Stencil 23 to reveal only the central plume motif and dots. Centre the stencil between the steps, and dab in paint.*

The tips of the finished motif are shaded with flame-like colours

Use a plumb line or spirit level to keep the torches straight

Mask off the torch so that only the top flame section is shown

4 *Position Stencil 24, the feather plume, above the last stencil, leaving a small gap. If you flip the plume and stencil from the other side, you can vary the look.*

5 *Paint in the torch (Stencil 27) in the spaces between the feather plumes. Then mask off the top section of the stencil, and fill in the gaps at the base of the steps.*

23

24

25

Trace the guidelines from this page onto the plastic stencil sheet. Cut along the vertical line of perforations that attaches the sheet to the book. Cut out and number each stencil. Place each one on card before removing any remaining infills with a scalpel.

27

26

28

Mayan & Aztec Variations

Mexican Pyramid:
Stencils 23, 24, 25, 27

You can create a dramatic focal point above a dado rail, a door, or a bookcase by stencilling this impressive pyramid

If space is available, increase the width of the base – the wider the base, the higher you can build up the pyramid to create a grand effect

Plume & Tula Stone Border: Stencils 23, 24, 27

Palm Border: Stencil 28

Plume Border: Stencil 24

Tula Stone Border: Stencil 23

Aztec Link Border: Stencils 17, 26

This is an example of how easy it is to mix motifs – in this case, Native American and Mayan & Aztec

Aztec Pyramid:
Stencils 24, 25, 27, 28

This complicated design re-creates the majesty of the pyramids, and is worth the effort; it works well as a wide border above a skirting-board

Combined with its mirror image, this design would create a large central motif for a floor rug; use the palm motif as a border

Toltec Step Border: Stencil 25

Toltec Square Border: Stencils 25, 26

Use this design for a quilt cover; you could also create the effect of a tiled surface by stencilling an entire dado area

Palm & Link Border: Stencils 26, 28

Try to keep a strong colour on the edges of any border to enclose and define the design

Mix & Match

MOST FOLK DESIGNS are based on geometrical shapes that are easy to repeat – horizontal and vertical lines, diamonds, squares, hand-drawn circles, chevrons – and for this reason, motifs from different parts of the world can be combined to produce your own unique designs. The following pages do not have a specific theme, but contain miscellaneous elements that can be used with any other stencil in the book. Feel free to combine any of the African stencils with each other, or perhaps with Native American designs, experiment with different colourways – and be as bold as the motifs!

The border of this rug is as easy to stencil as the frame shown below.

Pencil in vertical and horizontal lines at the midpoints of the frame

You can stretch the design to be as wide as you like – stencil two diamonds at the midpoints

1 For an unusual picture frame, position Stencil 29 in the top left corner, and mask off where it crosses the centre vertical line. Stencil, then rotate the stencil 180° and stencil again at the bottom right.

2 Pick up the stencil and place it in the upper right corner; mask the stencil corner, leaving enough of the border to fill the top of the frame. Stencil, then turn and repeat at the bottom of the frame.

3 Turn the stencil again, unmask the corner, and place in the top right corner. Mask the stencil where it meets the centre horizontal point, and stencil. Turn and repeat in the bottom left corner.

Mask the corner of the stencil and fill in any gaps on the frame with chevrons

Try using different colours for the chevrons and the corners

This design would work well on a mirror frame or on fabric place mats

4 Finish the frame by masking a small section of the stencil so that it fits in any remaining gaps. Make sure the chevrons go in the appropriate direction.

5 The finished frame is now ready for a photograph or another stencil design. It is always a good idea to measure the frame accurately and practise the design on a bit of lining or scrap paper first.

6 Once you have completed your frame, try filling it with a variety of different stencils. Shown here are Tropical African turtles (Stencil 2); most of the stencil was masked off to create the footprints.

29

30

A

B

Cut the holding bridges to create the outside frame
(30A) and the sheet of small motifs (30B).

31

32

Trace the
guidelines
from this page
onto the plastic
stencil sheet. Cut along
the vertical line of
perforations that attaches
the sheet to the book. Cut out
and number each stencil.
Place each one on card
before removing any
remaining infills
with a scalpel.

Mix & Match Variations

Squares & Diamonds Frieze: Stencil 29

Pointed Arrows: Stencil 32

African Panel: Stencils 5, 29

Mask off the chevron border and rotate the corner motif

Try highlighting the arrow point by using a strong, contrasting colour

These corner motifs can be used with any other border design

Use Stencil 30A for the solid background colour, then choose a contrasting colour for the small motifs (30B) and triangles (Stencil 31)

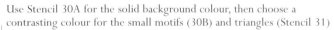

Diamond Arrow: Stencils 30a, 30b, 31

CHEVRON BORDER: STENCILS 29

ARROW BORDER: STENCILS 31, 32

LARGE PANEL: STENCILS 8B, 19A, 29, 30B

EAGLE DIAMOND: STENCILS 18, 21, 30A, 30B

This panel can be enlarged to create the look of a wall hanging – try using the Mayan & Aztec motifs in the centre

Stencil a diamond frame using Stencil 30A, dab in the eagle, then use 30B for the corner motifs

AZTEC MAZE: STENCILS 30A, 31, 32

This is a good design for a tile or a central pattern for a frame; if used on a quilt, try stitching between the painted areas

Attach 19A to the frame of Stencil 19, and dab in paint to create this motif

Art Editor **Wendy Bartlet**

Senior Editor **Christine Murdock**

Managing Art Editor **Steve Knowlden**

Managing Editor **Ian Whitelaw**

Production **Meryl Silbert**

DTP Designer **Matthew Greenfield**

*The authors would like to thank their families and good friends
for all their support — especially Clive and Fay.*

Dorling Kindersley would like to thank Andy Crawford, Steve Gorton,
Gary Ombler, and Colin Turner for photography

The Liquitex® acrylic paints used for the projects in this book are distributed in the UK by
Colart Fine Art & Graphics, Whitefriars Avenue, Harrow, Middlesex HA3 5RH

First published in Great Britain in 1997
by Dorling Kindersley Limited,
9 Henrietta Street, London WC2E 8PS
Copyright © 1997 Dorling Kindersley Limited, London
Visit us on the World Wide Web at http://www.dk.com

A CIP catalogue record for this book is available from the British Library.
ISBN 0-7513-1080-8

Reproduced by Bright Arts, Hong Kong
Printed and bound in Singapore by Imago